Parts, Pieces, & Particulars

A Primer for
Single Moms Raising Boys
and
Single Dads Raising Girls

Kay Clark Uhles

Kadabre Publishing

Parts, Pieces, & Particulars
A Primer for Single Moms Raising Boys and Single Dads Raising Girls
Kay Clark Uhles
Kadabre Publishing

Published by Kadabre Publishing
Copyright ©2020 Kay Clark Uhles
All rights reserved.

No part of this publication may be reproduced, stored in a retrieval system, or transmitted in any form or by any means, electronic, mechanical, photocopying, recording, scanning, or otherwise, except as permitted under Section 107 or 108 of the 1976 United States Copyright Act, without the prior written permission of the Publisher. Requests to the Publisher for permission should be addressed to Permissions Department, Kadabre Publishing, kadabrebooks@gmail.com.

Limit of Liability/Disclaimer of Warranty: While the publisher and author have used their best efforts in preparing this book, they make no representations or warranties with respect to the accuracy or completeness of the contents of this book and specifically disclaim any implied warranties of merchantability or fitness for a particular purpose. No warranty may be created or extended by sales representatives or written sales materials. The advice and strategies contained herein may not be suitable for your situation. You should consult with a professional where appropriate. Neither the publisher nor author shall be liable for any loss of profit or any other commercial damages, including but not limited to special, incidental, consequential, or other damages.

Cover and Interior design: Davis Creative, DavisCreative.com

Library of Congress Cataloging-in-Publication Data

Library of Congress Control Number: 2020921661

Kay Clark Uhles

Parts, Pieces, & Particulars: A Primer for Single Moms Raising Boys and Single Dads Raising Girls

ISBN: 978-1-7360476-0-6

Library of Congress subject headings:

1. FAM034010 FAMILY & RELATIONSHIPS / Parenting / Single Parent
   2 FAM034000 FAMILY & RELATIONSHIPS / Parenting / General

2020

Primer for Single Moms Raising Boys

DEDICATION

Parts, Pieces & Particulars is dedicated to single parents in general who do their best every day to care for the physical and emotional well-being of their children; and specifically, to those mothers and fathers who raise children of the opposite sex than that which they, themselves, were born.

I understand the struggles of knowing what to do in unfamiliar terrain.

My hat is off to you all!

Parts, Pieces, & Particulars

Table of Contents

Introduction vii

A Glossary of Parts and Pieces
  of the Male and Female Anatomy xi

Single Moms Raising Boys 1

Single Dads Raising Girls 33

LGBTQIA, TGNC 69

Parts, Pieces, & Particulars

Introduction

Growing up in a household of four daughters who were raised by a mother and grandmother, you can imagine the shock when my son was born. "What do I do with a boy?" was my first anesthesia-induced question to my husband in the recovery room. I had every faith that he knew. However, when my son was five, I divorced. My husband moved to another state and had little day-to-day contact with us from that point forward. Without his support and knowledge, again, questions came to me: How do I make a car noise? How do I tie a tie? How do I talk to my son about puberty? Hell! What happens to a boy in puberty? ***Parts, Pieces, and Particulars: A Primer for Single Moms Raising Boys and Single Dads Raising Girls*** answers these questions and more.

Parts, Pieces, & Particulars

This book discusses, in a concise manner, likes and dislikes of boys and girls as I knew them when I was raising my son and daughter. While addressing the development of cisgender boys and girls—that is, boys and girls who identify with their birth sex—this book, by no means, intends to stereotype gender roles. I recognize and accept that each child is an individual with their own likes and dislikes; therefore, no matter the sex of your child, I encourage you to read the entire book and apply the appropriate information for your own youngster.

Raising children of the opposite birth sex than you are accustomed to may be unfamiliar physical territory. Navigating a new topography, whether exploring a new city or bathing an infant's body which is unlike yours, takes some getting used to and may require some direction. Consider this your road map.

Parts, Pieces, & Particulars

While raising cisgender children has been the experience in my life, I have been touched by the raising of a transgender child. In ***Parts, Pieces, and Particulars,*** I have included, in a brief and succinct way, topics for LGBTQIA (lesbian, gay, bisexual, transgender, queer or questioning, intersex, and asexual) and TGNC (transgender and gender nonconforming) children. I am absolutely not an expert in the field. There is a myriad of resources available for guidance and support, some of which I have used and others which I have listed at the end of this book.

Recognition of LGBTQIA and TGNC people, including children, has increased over the last few years. And although, the United States and the world has made great strides in the recent past to show more understanding and inclusivity than ever before to LGBTQIA and TGNC children and adults, the terminology and etiquette may still be new to some. With the help of organizations like Out Boulder in Colorado and PFLAG, the Internet, and the resources I've listed at the end of this book, I have included the following not-so-exhaustive list of tips to help promote compassionate conversation with your LGBTQIA and TGNC child.

I hope sharing what I learned as I raised my son and daughter, and my awareness of the LGBTQIA and TGNC community, will answer your questions regarding the **Parts, Pieces, and Particulars** of your child.

Parts, Pieces, & Particulars

A Glossary of Parts and Pieces of the Male and Female Anatomy

areola: Circular pigmented area around the nipple

breasts/breast tissue: Fat, muscle, and ligament tissue on the chest, composed of an intricate network of blood vessels and glands specially designed for breastfeeding

cervix: Lower cylindrical portion of the uterus which separates the vagina from the rest of the uterus

clitoris (glans clitoris): Small sensory organ located toward the front of the vulva where the folds of the labia join

clitoral hood: Fold of skin that surrounds and protects the clitoris

ejaculation: Discharge of semen, usually containing sperm, from the penis

ejaculatory ducts: Canal in the male anatomy through which semen passes at the time of ejaculation

Parts, Pieces, & Particulars

erection: Lengthening and hardening of the penis during sexual arousal

fallopian tubes: Muscular tubes in the female reproductive system connecting the ovaries to the uterus

hymen: Membrane of tissue covering the external vaginal opening

labia: Two pairs of skin flaps that surround the vaginal opening

labia majora: Fleshy outer lips on either side of the vaginal opening

labia minora: Inner lips inside the outer lips

menstruation (period): Blood and tissues released from the inner lining of the uterus on a monthly basis, lasting from two to seven days. A monthly cycle for an adult woman may range from twenty-one to thirty-five days but may vary in teen girls

mons pubis (pubic mound): Fleshy tissue over the pubic bone, usually covered in pubic hair in adulthood

Parts, Pieces, & Particulars

nipple: Rounded and often raised tissue on the surface of the breast in the female anatomy from which milk drains to feed a baby

ovaries: Two oval-shaped organs located to the upper right and left of the uterus that produce female sex hormones (such as estrogen and progesterone), and produce, store, and release eggs into the fallopian tubes during the process called "ovulation"

ovulation: Female reproductive process by which eggs are released into the fallopian tubes

ovum (Latin: "egg"): Female reproductive cell released by the ovaries and when fertilized by male sperm produces an embryo

penis: Male external reproductive organ

perineum: Tissue between the vaginal opening or scrotum and the anus

Parts, Pieces, & Particulars

premenstrual syndrome (PMS): Physical and emotional symptoms which may occur around seven days before monthly menstruation begins. Symptoms may include:

- acne
- bloating
- tiredness
- trouble handling stress
- backaches
- sore breasts
- headaches
- constipation
- diarrhea
- food cravings
- depression
- irritability

prostate: Walnut-sized gland located just in front of the rectum that secretes fluid to nourish and protect sperm

semen (seminal fluid): Male organic fluid that contains sperm cells and is released through the penis during ejaculation

seminal vesicles (seminal glands): Pair of glands located within the male pelvis that secrete fluid to contribute to the normal functioning of semen

scrotum: Sac that surrounds and protects the testes

Parts, Pieces, & Particulars

spermatozoa (sperm): Male sex cells produced by the testes and carry a man's genetic material and fertilize the female ovum during the act of sex

testes (testicles): Pair of external oval-shaped organs located in the scrotum behind the penis that produce sperm and the male hormone, testosterone

urethra: Opening above the vagina in females which carries urine from the bladder to the outside of the body; and located in males at the tip of the penis which transports semen and urine

uterus (womb): Muscular sac located in the middle of the female pelvic cavity which houses the fetus during pregnancy

vagina: Canal in the female reproductive system connecting the vulva with the uterus

vas deferens: Muscular tube in the male reproductive system that transports sperm to the ejaculatory ducts

vulva: External genitalia of the female reproductive organs, including the labia majora and labia minora

Single Moms Raising Boys

To be a mother of a son is one of the most important things you can do to change the world. Raise them to respect women, raise them to stand up for others, raise them to care for the earth, raise them to be kind, compassionate and honest. If you do these things you are raising a leader— someone that will affect the lives of countless people with their morality. Their future wife and children will thank you...

— Shannon L. Alder

Parts, Pieces, & Particulars

At birth, hormones discharge into the placenta which cause the baby boy's penis, scrotum, and breasts to swell.

Whether for reasons of avoiding baby's exposure to chemicals or contributing to landfills, cloth diapers are experiencing a comeback. Many cloth diapers are extra-long, especially for newborns. Fold extra cloth of diapers to the front for baby boys. Point the penis down.

Primer for Single Moms Raising Boys

Circumcision is the removal of the foreskin from the glans, or tip, of the penis. Stemming from religious ritual and family traditions, circumcisions are often performed on newborn boys.

The decision to circumcise a newborn male is personal and requires in-depth investigation into the incidences of pain for the infant and available anesthesia, long- and short-term care of the circumcised or uncircumcised penis, and the necessity, if not done at birth, to circumcise older males in the future. Libraries and bookstores offer many books on the topic. Consult your physician for guidance.

Parts, Pieces, & Particulars

When bathing uncircumcised boys, without retracting the foreskin, gently clean all creases and crevices using soap and water.

Spontaneous erections are normal in baby boys and regularly occur during diaper changes.

Primer for Single Moms Raising Boys

During diaper changes and bath time when baby boys are exposed to cooler air, they may spontaneously pee. When removing the diaper, keep the penis covered with a diaper or washcloth to avoid an unexpected shower.

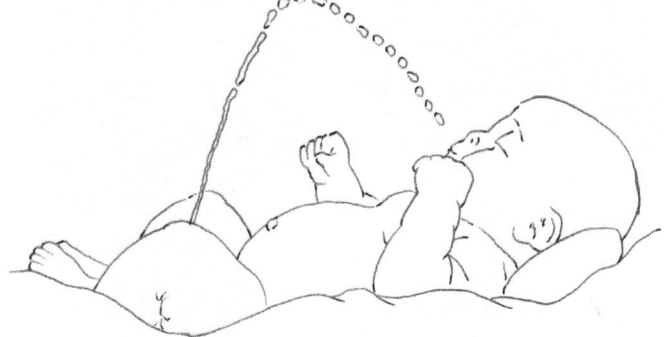

Parts, Pieces, & Particulars

Initially, little boys may learn to urinate sitting down. That doesn't mean they are leaning toward feminism.

Potty chairs are equipped with guards at the front of the seat to prevent accidental splashes. Boys will probably stand later, once the practice has been modeled.

Primer for Single Moms Raising Boys

The age for potty training depends on the child. And it probably won't happen until the child—not the parent—is ready. Some signs to watch for:

- If he becomes interested in body parts.
- If he pretends to go to the bathroom on the potty.
- If he pretends to wipe.
- If his diaper remains dry for more than an hour.
- If he watches you or brothers/sisters go to the bathroom.

Training boys to stand to urinate may not be necessary until they begin preschool and witness other little boys at the toilet.

Parts, Pieces, & Particulars

If you decide to train your son to stand while urinating, strategize to keep misses down. Place a flushable and floatable object in the water, such as a section of toilet paper or breakfast cereal—e.g., Cheerios—as a target.

Even with the best no-miss strategies, with boys, toilet misses and messes are inevitable.

Boys shake after urinating;
they don't wipe.

Primer for Single Moms Raising Boys

For safety concerns, do not send young boys into public restrooms alone. Family facilities are provided in many restaurants, malls, and other popular establishments.

Men's rooms are all about business. At all times, eyes are cast forward and at chest level, with a respectable distance kept between occupied urinals.

Parts, Pieces, & Particulars

Because social norms in a men's room are different from a women's room, on the first visit to a public men's room, consider having your son accompanied by a trusted adult male.

Although many factors determine height, a boy's height doubled at the age of two years may predict an approximate final adult height.

Boys tend to get more ear infections than girls.

Loud farts can be funny in the right place at the right time.

Primer for Single Moms Raising Boys

Making a car noise (or starship or rocket or transformer noise) may not be your cup of tea, but give it a try. It may bring giggles to you and your son, if not an acceptable car sound!

- Close your lips,
- Press your bottom lip tightly onto your bottom gum,
- Build up saliva at the back of your throat; and,
- Make a "V" sound.

Voilà! It's a motor!

Parts, Pieces, & Particulars

Your boy may be naturally competitive and physical or he may be naturally noncompetitive and relational. Get to know him. He's perfect!

※

Show up to his events!

※

Boys cry too. It's okay.

Primer for Single Moms Raising Boys

Pets may be beneficial for all children, but perhaps especially for boys. Boys may learn responsibility, empathy, and sympathy for others through caring for a dog, cat, hamster, rat, or goldfish. Pet ownership and care may also advance a child's self-esteem.

A caveat:

Be careful about bringing home six rats from grade school to care for over spring break. They reproduce quickly!

Parts, Pieces, & Particulars

Don't just raise a good son; raise a good husband,

father, citizen, and steward of the earth.

Raise a good man!

—

Make a game out of cleaning with your son.

Whoever gets the most clutter in their basket

in five minutes wins!

—

Teach your son how to do his laundry

to avoid catastrophes, like reds fading and

creating pink underwear for him.

Primer for Single Moms Raising Boys

Teaching your son how to cook and/or bake builds confidence and creates a bond between mother and son. His future partner in life will thank you!

Do not pin the title of "man of the house" on your young son. This title comes with responsibilities. Reassure him that Mom is in charge.

Do things and talk about things your son likes. Legos, video games, cars, space adventures, dolls, or makeup—make an effort to learn his favorite things.

Parts, Pieces, & Particulars

Young boys may delight in their first fishing trip that is simple and fun. A still-water lake or slow-moving stream is perfect. Easy-to-use equipment includes an ordinary pole and fishing line, a hook, bobber, weight, and worms.

Of course, don't forget the folding chairs, snacks, drinks, and sunscreen for a day of fun!

Primer for Single Moms Raising Boys

To put a worm on the hook, start at the band, or broadest part, of the worm. Thread the worm onto a small hook two or three times, covering the tip of the hook completely, leaving enough of the worm to dangle and attract fish (but not too much for the fish to take nibbles and escape).

Don't name the worms; they will be harder to thread onto the hook.

The weight (a lead piece tied or clamped onto the fishing line to help your bait sink to certain depths) should be set so the bait floats just above the bottom of the lake or stream. Toss the line into the water and wait for the bobber (a float which stays on the surface of the water and is a visual indicator of a bite) to move. When a fish is on the line, swing the pole and line over to dry land, hold the fish tightly, and remove the hook. For catch and release, return the fish to the water.

Parts, Pieces, & Particulars

For queasy fisher-moms or for practice before hitting the lake, fish off the porch.
Attach string to a stick. Tie a paper clip to the other end of the string. "Hook" a gummy worm or a piece of spaghetti to the paper clip and hang the stick over the porch railing.
Goldfish crackers may be the catch of the day!

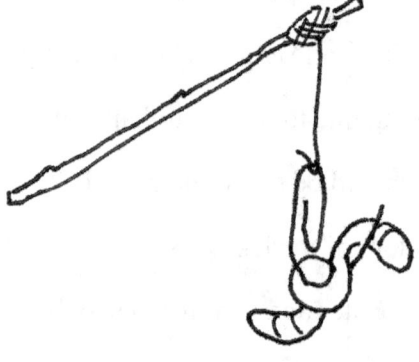

Primer for Single Moms Raising Boys

If possible, help your son build or maintain a relationship with his father.

There are some eighteen different ways to tie a necktie. An adult male's choice of necktie knots may signal to the world around him power, trust, approachability, refinement, or any number of things. A young boy does not need a subliminal gimmick; the simplest ties, such as a clip-on tie or the everyday Simple Knot, may be appropriate.

Parts, Pieces, & Particulars

Tying a "Simple" knot

1. Flip the collar up and button at the neck
2. Facing your son and with the broad side of the tie in your dominant hand, drape the seam side of the tie away from the collar; adjust the length starting with the slender tip just above the fourth button from the bottom of the shirt
3. With the nondominant hand, hold the narrow end about three inches down from the neck
4. Wide end goes under the narrow end.
5. With the dominant hand, pass the wide end over the top and around the narrow end, stopping at the back
6. Pass the broad end up through the V that is formed and tuck the broad end down through the loop
7. Tighten by holding the slender side and slipping the knot up snuggly to the neck
8. Smooth the knot and adjust the length if necessary
9. Turn the collar down.

Primer for Single Moms Raising Boys

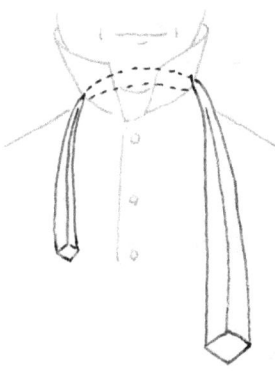
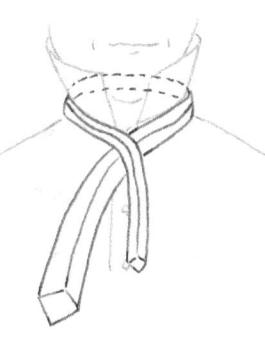
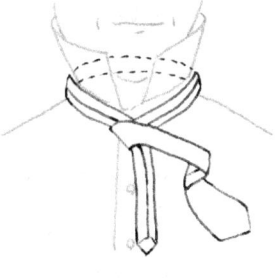
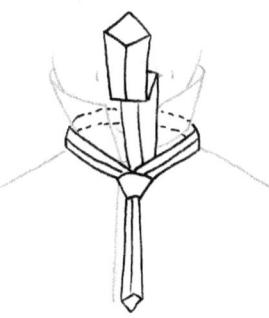
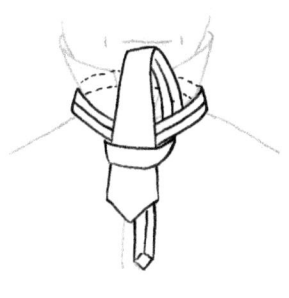

Parts, Pieces, & Particulars

You might take away all the guns from your boy; but if he wants a gun to play with, he will create it with his hand, a paper-towel core, a piece of paper—anything.

※

Participation in sports is not war. It is a social act for parents and kids.

※

If there are no male friends or family members close by to be a role-model for your son, register him in an organization that models manhood.

Primer for Single Moms Raising Boys

Underweight males may see themselves negatively.

—

Boys should not be surprised by puberty and its effects on the body.

—

Uninformed boys may become alarmed and fearful of spontaneous erections and wet dreams. Inform your son in advance about the upcoming events of puberty.

Parts, Pieces, & Particulars

Informative discussions of pubescence may be difficult but necessary. You may decide to start these conversations when your son is between the ages of ten and twelve. Ask your pediatrician, trusted male friend, or family member to speak to you and your son. Books at your local library can also help with these discussions.

Primer for Single Moms Raising Boys

During the "birds-and-bees" talk, it's important that you share your values and beliefs concerning the subject with your son. Listen to his values, beliefs, and desires as well.

Reading a book is nice—a frank discussion after he reads each chapter is priceless.

Share your desires for his sexual health.

Tip: Before starting the birds-and-bees talk with your son, consider taking a short road trip, getting your speed up to sixty miles per hour, locking the car doors, and driving on a bridge over fast moving water to keep your son from jumping out.

Talk!

Parts, Pieces, & Particulars

Sleeping boys, ages twelve to eighteen, often experience erotic dreams with erections and a spontaneous flow of clear or creamy fluid. These events are called "wet dreams."

When boys begin to move into puberty, their closets, rooms, shoes, and socks—hell, the whole house—may (will) smell like a locker room.

Tender and swollen nipples may occur with some boys during puberty.

Primer for Single Moms Raising Boys

Facial hair often develops in boys between the ages of sixteen and twenty years old; However, some boys may develop mustaches much earlier.

Manual shaving with a razor or electric shaving are available for your son.

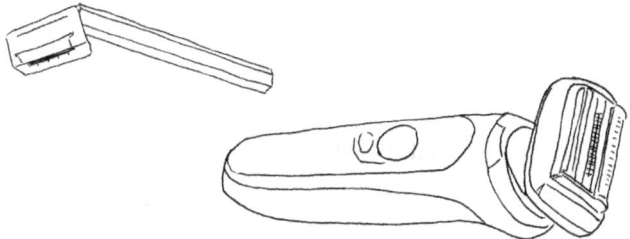

Parts, Pieces, & Particulars

For manual shaving, to reduce razor burn, use very warm (not hot) water, a wash cloth, soap, and shaving cream.

- Fill the sink with warm water.
- Using upward motions, soften the beard by lathering the face with soap and a cloth, rinse.
- Soak the cloth again in the water and hold on the face for a couple of minutes.
- Work shaving cream into lather in circular motions over beard.
- Dip the razor into the water and grasp the handle firmly.
- Shave in the direction of the growth of the whiskers in a systematic fashion to avoid missing areas, dipping the razor in water periodically.
- Using the free, dry hand, pull the skin taut against the razor just outside the lathered area. Be sure to lift the blade off the skin completely to avoid accidental cuts.
- Soak the cloth in cool water and place over the freshly shaved face to close the pores.
- Going against the grain, gently feel the skin for any missed patches of whiskers.

Tips for manual shaving

- Dull, dirty razorblades, and ill-prepared beards cause most shaving mishaps.
- Replace old blades in a manual razor.
- Single-blade razors irritate facial skin less than double-blade razors; however, double-blade razors may give a closer shave.

Electric shavers should be used on dry skin only. Although soaking the beard with a very warm, moist cloth makes whiskers stand up, cornstarch or powder should be used to dry the face before shaving. In circular movements, and going against the direction of growth, start at the hinge of the jaw and move upward, using the free hand to pull taut the skin to be shaved.

Parts, Pieces, & Particulars

Tips for electric shaving

- Pivoting-head electric shavers maneuver around angles and bones more easily.
- Clean heads in an electric shaver regularly.
- Diet, stress, temperature, and humidity may affect resilience of the skin and the degree of razor burn.

Aftershave may irritate the skin. Aloe Vera gel is a natural way to soothe and moisturize tender facial skin. A cool washcloth may also help soothe the skin.

Primer for Single Moms Raising Boys

As mothers raising sons, we have the power to change the trajectory of not only our own sons' lives, but also of the culture at large.

— Melia Keeton Digby

Single Dads Raising Girls

One of the greatest things about daughters is how they adored you when they were little; how they rushed into your arms with electric delight and demanded that you watch everything they do and listen to everything they say. Those memories will help you through less joyous times when their adoration is replaced by embarrassment or annoyance and they don't want you to see what they are doing or hear what they are saying. And yet, you will adore your daughter every day of her life, hoping to be valued again, but realizing how fortunate you were even if you only get what you already got.

– Michael Josephson

Parts, Pieces, & Particulars

Just prior to birth, hormones naturally flow into the infant's system, causing redness and swelling of the baby girl's breasts and genitals. A whitish discharge from the baby girl's breasts may occur.

Although a blood-tinged vaginal discharge is common in girl babies within the first few days after birth, call your pediatrician if there is blood in her diaper.

Because girls are more susceptible to urinary tract infections than boys, change your daughter's soiled diaper immediately.

Primer for Single Dads Raising Girls

Disposable diapers or cloth diapers? Cloth diapers are experiencing a comeback. You may choose cloth diapers to protect your baby girl's bum from chemicals or protect the environment from waste. Many cloth diapers are extra-long, especially for newborns. Fold extra cloth of diapers to the back for baby girls.

Lay the baby on a dry, flat surface protected by an extra diaper or a changing pad (cloth or disposable). If not protected and your baby girl pees during a diaper change, everything under her will be wet and need to be changed.

To change the diaper, hold onto the baby girl's legs by the feet and ankles so that she can be easily lifted for slipping the diaper under her.

Parts, Pieces, & Particulars

Wet-Only Diaper Changes

For wet diapers, clean the diaper area with a little water or a mild, soap-free, unscented baby cleansing product, and a clean washcloth, cotton pad, or alcohol-free baby wipes. Always wipe front to back to avoid urinary infections. Spread the labia and gently clean all creases, crevices, and the perineal area. Do not prod for dirt in places which cannot be seen!

For messy diaper changes, girls require a little more care than boys. Gently clean the vaginal area first. Then wipe front to back to avoid spreading feces into vulnerable parts. From there, moving to the outside, clean everything away from creases in the labia. Don't forget to check the mid- and lower-back region as poo often gravitates upwards.

Primer for Single Dads Raising Girls

Girls naturally have a whitish vaginal discharge.
Don't try to wash it away.

Some girls love bubble baths, but sometimes
bubble bath solutions can cause vaginitis, urinary
tract infections, or mild irritation.
A mild baby shampoo may produce bubbles
with less irritations.

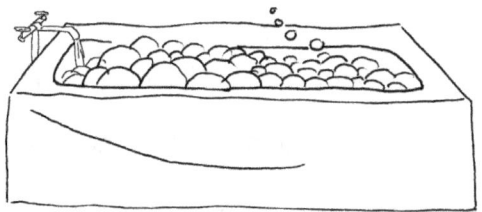

Although many factors determine height,
a girl's height at the age of eighteen months may
predict an approximate final adult height.

Parts, Pieces, & Particulars

"What's that?" the question often asked by little girls when confronted with the awareness of their father's penis can be answered with the correct term. "Penis," pure and simple, answers her question. She may become afraid that her penis is missing, in which case,

"You are a girl. You have a vagina,"

would be appropriate.

Convincing your daughter she does not have the correct anatomic equipment to stand to urinate may be difficult and messy after watching Daddy stand and aim.

If she insists, train her to sit backwards, straddling the bowl and facing the tank.

Sooner or later she will accept she is a girl and must sit.

Crying cleanses the soul. Listening and reflecting the feelings behind the tears may open communication between father and daughter.

Underweight girls see themselves as average weight.

Brushing hair can be difficult and tear-producing. To remove tangles, hold the hair firmly, close to the scalp, to avoid pulling the hair. Brush the ends first, then move upward.

Parts, Pieces, & Particulars

What's the difference between a pigtail, a ponytail, and a braid?

And who cares? Your daughter does!
- A ponytail is one tail held at the center and back of the head. The ponytail can be placed high or low on the head.
- Pigtails are two tails along both sides of a center part. Each pigtail can be fastened high or just below the earlobes.
- Braids can be created with a ponytail, or pigtails, or flat on the head.

To create a ponytail:

- Remove all tangles. Brush all hair into one "tail" centered at the back of the head.
- Keeping hair as smooth as possible, at the scalp, secure with hair elastic (also called, "ponytail holder" or "hair tie"). Barrettes, to fit the thickness of your daughter's hair, can also be used to secure the ponytail.
- Do not use a rubber band as hair will become broken and/or tangled!

To create pigtails:

- Part the hair down the middle of the head.
- Comb each side back toward or behind the ear and to the desired height.
- Keep the hair as smooth as possible.
- Pigtails can be fastened with hair ties/…elastics above or below the ears.

Parts, Pieces, & Particulars

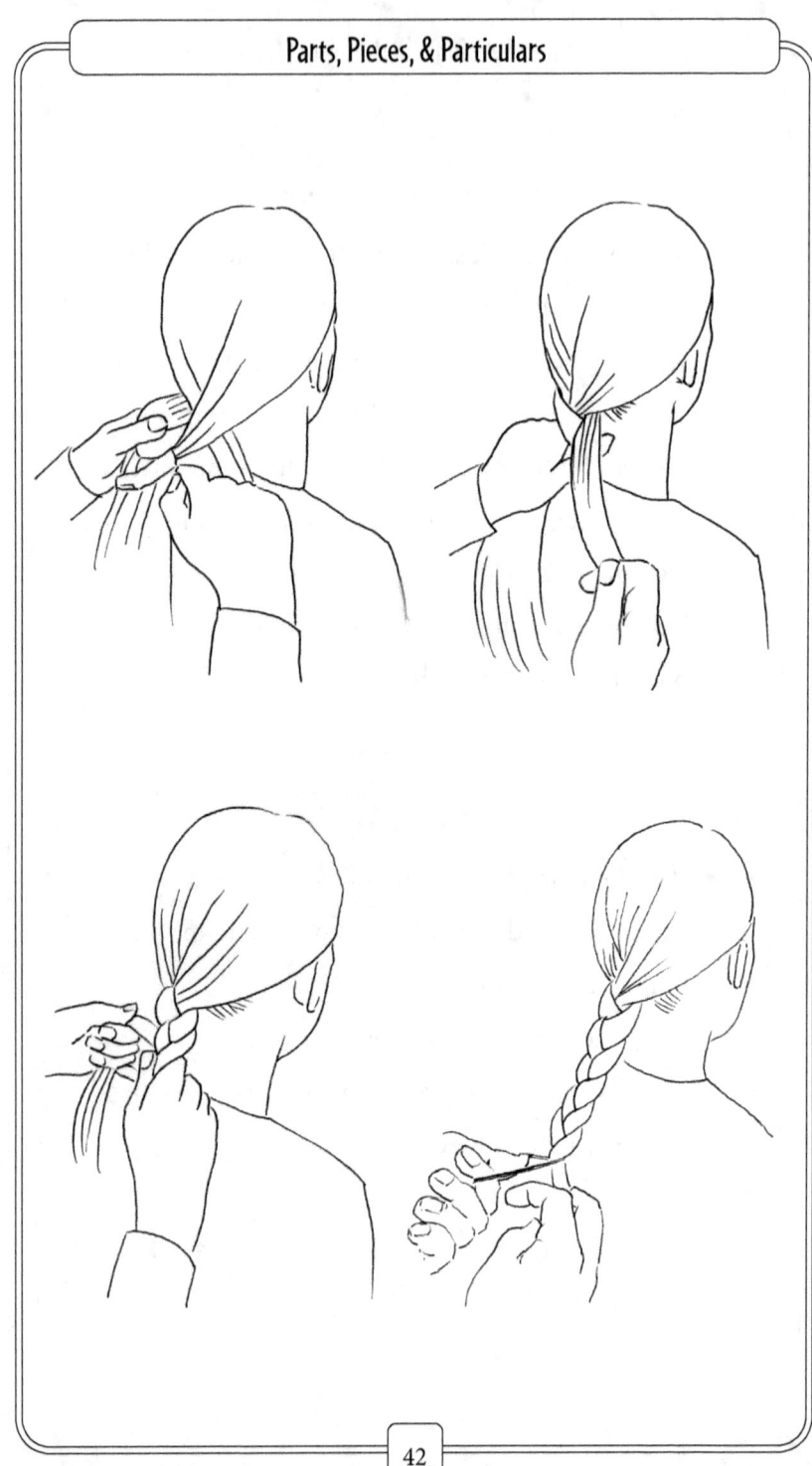

Braiding hair:

There are several types of braids, from elegant and fancy to everyday and simple. Let's start with the simple ones. Braids can be created as a ponytail or pigtails.

- Comb and smooth the hair back for a ponytail or pigtails. Fastening at this point is optional. If not fastened, pull the hair smoothly to the nape of the neck.
- Divide the section (whether ponytail or pigtail) into three equal parts.
- Keeping hair as smooth as possible, separating each part with your fingers, cross the right section over the middle section. Pull tight.
- Cross the left side over the new middle section.
- Repeat until all hair is braided. Fasten with a hair tie.
- Don't forget the wonders of YouTube demonstration videos if you have trouble. You might consider practicing with yarn taped to a table.

Braid long hair before swimming and motorcycle or convertible rides to prevent tangles.

Parts, Pieces, & Particulars

Chewing gum caught in your daughter's hair got you down?

No need to cut it out. Here are several home remedies for easy removal:

- Apply an ice pack or ice cubes wrapped in a cloth to the affected hair. Wait for five to fifteen minutes or until the gum hardens and breaks off.
- Dip the gum-stuck hair into a cup of Coca-Cola or vinegar for a few minutes (Warming the vinegar may speed the process). Comb through hair with a wide-toothed comb or pick to remove the gum.
- Directly apply a small amount of creamy peanut butter, mayonnaise, vegetable oil, or olive oil on the affected hair, rub gently, and shampoo.

While waiting for any of the above remedies to work, pass the time by singing three verses of "This Old Man."

Primer for Single Dads Raising Girls

This old man, he played one,
He played knick-knack on my thumb;
With a knick-knack paddywhack,
Give a dog a bone,
This old man came rolling home.
This old man, he played two,
He played knick-knack on my shoe;
With a knick-knack paddywhack,
Give a dog a bone,
This old man came rolling home.
This old man, he played three,
He played knick-knack on my knee;
With a knick-knack paddywhack,
Give a dog a bone,
This old man came rolling home.

Parts, Pieces, & Particulars

Paint her nails.

But be prepared, there will come a time when she wants to paint your nails.

Primer for Single Dads Raising Girls

Your daughter, one day, may emerge from her bedroom wearing atrocious combinations of clothing (in your opinion)—perhaps even everything in her closet! Experimentation with clothes, styles, and appearances is normal. Let her try it all! She's trying on and trying out her growing personality.

She will one day settle on a style more in line with female models in her life (probably).

Parts, Pieces, & Particulars

Set a good example for good eating habits. Anorexia and bulimia continue to affect young girls today. Building your daughter's self-esteem can eliminate eating disorders as she matures. Self-image is the reflection of the mirror she sees in your eyes.

Teasing about weight and the appearance of your daughter's body sends a negative image.

Attending her school events and extracurricular activities may be one simple act to send the message that she matters.

Rock out to her music in the car.

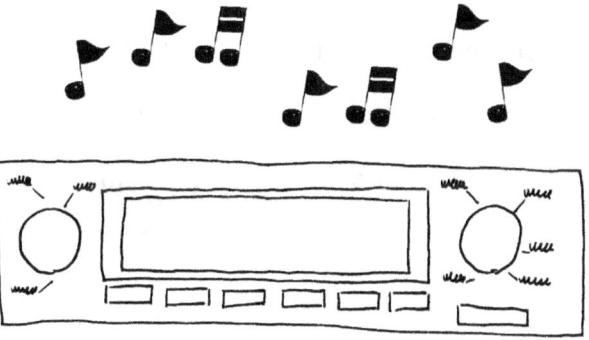

Parts, Pieces, & Particulars

Do not send your young daughter into a women's restroom alone. Many malls, restaurants, and other public facilities provide family restrooms to accommodate parents and children.

Contrary to popular belief, STDs (sexually transmitted diseases) do not survive outside of warm, moist areas and are not transmitted on toilet seats. If queasy about placing your daughter on a public seat, though, line the seat with provided toilet-seat liners or fold toilet paper over the seat to ease the concerned mind.

Primer for Single Dads Raising Girls

Some girls, even women, have difficulty urinating outdoors. If it is necessary, however, your young daughter may need your help in holding her in a squatting position in the woods.

Don't laugh when a tween girl expresses an opinion on current events, boys, sex, double standards, climate change, harassment, #MeToo, politics, recriminalization of abortions— anything. Listen to her point of view. Listening and agreeing are two different things.

Parts, Pieces, & Particulars

You may recall bygone days when your daughter tells you of an experience. Remember: Her experience is different than yours. Lecturing, distrusting, diminishing, and/or doubting your daughter's experiences, concerns and/or beliefs, may define your future relationship with her.

Be wrong sometimes.
Admit it. Apologize.

Primer for Single Dads Raising Girls

If possible, help your daughter build or maintain a relationship with her mother.

While fatherly hugs for tween girls are acceptable, the once-proper slaps on your little girl's bottom are now taboo. Keep your hands off.

Parts, Pieces, & Particulars

The average age for menstruation to begin is between nine and twelve. Before this happens, though, breasts will begin to develop, her body will change shape, and she may develop acne. This is your sign to be prepared!

Age ten to the time breast development begins is a good time to explain your daughter's future menstruation to her. If girls are not told explicitly about their bodily changes during puberty, they may be alarmed, even afraid of dying, when they first start their periods. For help, consider talking to a physician, a trusted woman friend/relative, and/or check out a book at your library.

Primer for Single Dads Raising Girls

The "birds-and-bees" talk can be uncomfortable, both for father and daughter; however, it's important that you share your values and beliefs with her concerning the subject.

Having her read a book is nice—frank discussions after she reads each chapter is priceless. Share your values and your desires for her sexual health.

Listen to her values, beliefs, and desires.

Parts, Pieces, & Particulars

Be prepared! As you and your daughter cruise the feminine products aisle, you will have to make a decision or two: Panty-liners or mini-pads or maxi-pads or pads with wings or oversized or long pads for nighttime.

Bottom line: Stock up on sanitary pads for your daughter before she begins to menstruate. Consider buying a discreet pouch so that she can carry pads in her purse or bookbag.

Keep in mind that now, in the era of the Internet, purchases of feminine products can be done online, averting the embarrassment of standing in the feminine products aisle.

Feminine pads should be changed at least every three to four hours depending on your daughter's flow.

Eventually, your daughter may want to switch to tampons. Encourage her to become accustomed to her menstruation cycle with pads first.

Parts, Pieces, & Particulars

For proper hygiene and safety of tampon use:
- Change tampon often.
- Use only one tampon at a time.
- Wash hands before and after inserting tampon.
- Alternate tampon use with feminine pad use.
- Use tampon during active menstrual phase only and remove tampon at end of period.
- Use a fresh tampon at bedtime; remove or replace with new tampon upon awakening.

Primer for Single Dads Raising Girls

For "that time of month," you and your daughter might consider period panties for a sense of confidence and hygiene. These leak-preventing panties are stylish for a teen—they are not grandma panties! They come in an array of colors and styles that your daughter will feel comfortable in: from briefs to boy shorts and sports styles to hip-huggers and thongs. Select high, medium, or low absorbency based on menstrual flow. Look for cotton insides that create breathable comfort.

Some brands recommend the additional use of panty liners or pads, some do not; some panties can be reused, some cannot. Shopper's choice.

Parts, Pieces, & Particulars

Lest you think you know all there is to know about feminine hygiene products, check this out! Period cups can be inserted into the vagina by a menstrual neophyte and, if inserted properly, may replace pads or liners. While tampons and pads need to be replaced in a matter of hours, a period cup can be left in longer, depending on flow. Look for wallet-friendly and eco-friendly reusable cups—they may last for years. Be sure to follow package directions for care and cleaning.

Primer for Single Dads Raising Girls

Girls may experience cramps during their periods. A heating pad and perhaps Naproxen sodium may offer some relief. "Father of the Year" goes to the dad who offers chocolate and/or salty snacks to their menstruating daughter.

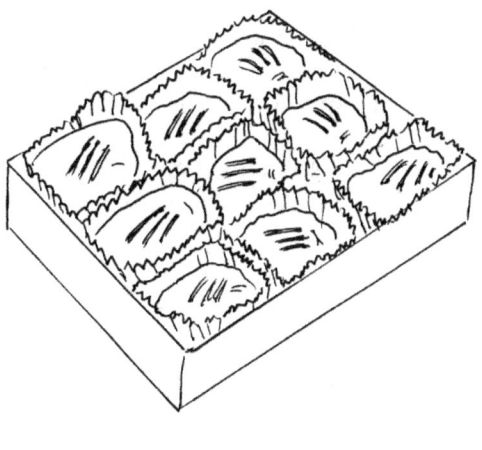

Abnormal periods, lasting less than two or more than seven days, pain, or excessive menstrual bleeding may indicate gynecological problems and the need for a visit to the doctor.

Avoid fragranced feminine hygiene products that can cause irritations and reactions. Feminine odors are normal and should not be masked with perfumes, only cleansed regularly.

Medical experts recommend that a girl's first gynecological appointment is between thirteen and fifteen years old.

Being nervous for the first gynecological exam is normal; however, a female gynecologist may help your daughter relax during the appointment. Assure your daughter that the exam is normal and there may not be a pelvic exam until after the age of twenty-one; although, there may be a urinalysis required. Rescheduling may be necessary if your daughter is on her period. Discuss visit details and requirements with your physician's office.

Parts, Pieces, & Particulars

Don't just raise a good daughter. Raise a good wife and mother, a sensitive and caring human being, a responsible citizen—a great woman!

Puppy love is real. Remember? When/if it happens to your daughter, take a deep breath and then, if needed, find a parent support group to help you through it.

Primer for Single Dads Raising Girls

Although, teenage "sex-perimenting" has been around forever, sexting (the exchange of sexual- or erotic-based photos or texts via digital devices) is a phenomenon of the Internet generations. Research varies widely on the pros/cons of sexting; i.e., legal consequences and emotional complications. Become familiar with electronic parental controls on cell phones and computers.

Parts, Pieces, & Particulars

Shaving her legs for the first time, a girl may find it easier and safer in the bathtub. Bath soaps and shower gels may be used in lieu of shaving cream to lather the legs for a smooth glide of the razor upwards from the ankle to the knee. Choices of razors include bi-directional blades which allow for the shaving in both directions, up and down, without lifting the handle. The need for safety around the shins, knees, and Achilles tendon should be stressed no matter which blade she uses. Blot dry and apply moisturizing lotion when finished.

Primer for Single Dads Raising Girls

To shave under arms, raise the arm high, tightening and flattening the armpit indentations. Lather, shave, rinse. Repeat.

To avoid the clown look and to teach your young daughter the fine art (and tasteful use) of makeup of which you approve, throw an in-home or virtual makeup party with her friends! You may endear yourself to your daughter forever or perhaps keep her close to home as she grows into a young women.
In the alternative, schedule an appointment with a cosmetics consultant or makeup artist. Kudos if you decide to join in! Just be sure to take pictures to share with family and friends.

Parts, Pieces, & Particulars

Dad. He can play like a kid,

give advice like a friend,

and protect like a bodyguard.

– Unknown

LGBTQIA, TGNC

I think what you're seeing is a profound recognition on the part of the American people that gays and lesbians and transgender persons are our brothers, our sisters, our children, our cousins, our friends, our co-workers, and that they've got to be treated like every other American. And I think that principle will win out.

– Barack Obama

Parts, Pieces, & Particulars

Gender labels throughout history have been stamped on at birth according to the doctor's declaration: "It's a boy!" or "It's a girl!" Today, gender is not put into just two boxes and is not defined by the medical community, nor by parents. It is a spectrum of many hues: Neutrois, agender, nonbinary, genderqueer, androgynes, bigender, bois, demigender, gender fluid, gender-nonconforming, and so on. Gender terms continue to evolve to this day.

LGBTQIA, TGNC

Kids explore their gender and may decide they do not identify with the sex of their birth.

If the family decides to support transgender surgery, introduction of hormones may be required before pubescent development begins. Risks exist, however. Expert guidance is needed.

Parts, Pieces, & Particulars

Upon finding out that a child is LGBTQIA or TGNC, parents may react differently, either positively or negatively. They may be overcome with happiness that their child shared the information with them, with relief that they are now open to finding support to help their child along their path, with excitement for their child's self-awareness; or they may be overcome with fear of the unknown, sadness for the perceived struggles they may face, or devastation. Parents may choose to find a support group to help both themselves and the child with present and future challenges.

LGBTQIA, TGNC

LGBTQIA and TGNC children may be referred to in a myriad of terms: gender expansive, gender nonconforming, gender creative, gay, lesbian, or transgender to name just a few.

Be your child's greatest supporter and advocate. Love them unconditionally.

Parts, Pieces, & Particulars

Pronouns are a personal preference. While some prefer she, he, her, him, hers, his, et cetera; others may use, ze, hir, and hirs; and still others may use ze (sometimes spelled zie) and hir or xe and xer; they may also prefer a different name than that given at birth. If your child identifies as gender expansive, learn and use the preferred gender pronouns and names.

Calling someone a pronoun, like "he," "she," or "it," may be seen as disrespectful and invalidating identity. The term "tranny" offends.

LGBTQIA, TGNC

Don't assume.

Ask your child and others, directly, what pronouns to use in reference to them.

Asking others personal questions, like, "Have you had surgery?" or "What are you really?" is inappropriate. Stand up for your child if you hear such questions directed to them.

Parts, Pieces, & Particulars

If you use the wrong pronoun,

apologize and move on.

Ask your family and friends to be respectful of

your child's identity.

LGBTQIA, TGNC

Transphobia refers to the hatred or fear of people who do not conform to society's expectation of gender roles. Confront transphobia when you see it or hear it.

Join a gender non-conforming play group for support and fun!

Parts, Pieces, & Particulars

Love is love.

It takes courage to grow up and

become who you really are.

– e.e. cummings

LGBTQIA Resources

Family Equality Council

The GLBT National Help Center

Human Rights Campaign (HRC)

Parents, Family & Friends of Lesbians and Gays,

Gays & Lesbian Advocates & Defenders (GLAD)

Lambda Legal Defense and Education Fund

National LGBT Bar Association

Transgender Law Center

Advocates for Informed Choice (AIC)

Gay, Lesbian & Straight Educators Network

Gay and Lesbian Medical Association (GLMA)

National Gay and Lesbian Chamber of Commerce (NGLCC)

National Organization of Gay and Lesbian Scientists and Technical Professionals (NOGLSTP)

National Gay Pilots Association

Parts, Pieces, & Particulars

National Lesbian & Gay Journalists Association (NLGJA)

Pride at Work

Out & Equal Workplace Advocates

American Veterans for Equal Rights (AVER)

OutServe-SLDN

Gay & Lesbian Association of Retiring Persons (GLARP)

Services & Advocacy for Gay, Lesbian, Bisexual Transgender Elders (SAGE)

https://www.ncbi.nlm.nih.gov/pubmed/24826822, retrieved 9/1/19

https://newsnetwork.mayoclinic.org/discussion/childs-height-at-age-2-may-predict-dult-height/

https://www.mayoclinic.org/healthy-lifestyle/childrens-health/expert-answers/child-growth/faq-20057990

https://pflag.org

Parts, Pieces, & Particulars

With much gratitude to:

David and Breck, whom I parented with love.

Leslie Spillman, RN, PA, MPAS

Writing group:

Lisa

Louise

Nancy

Petey

Vicki

Focus Group:

Andrea

Sarah

Jamie

Kayla

Kay can be reached at:

KayClarkUhles.com

mindwise.soulworks@gmail.com

https://www.facebook.com/Kay-Clark-Uhles-Journeys

https://www.linkedin.com/in/kay-clark-uhles

www.ingramcontent.com/pod-product-compliance
Lightning Source LLC
Chambersburg PA
CBHW072207100526
44589CB00015B/2403